The Official MANCHESTER CITY Annual 2014

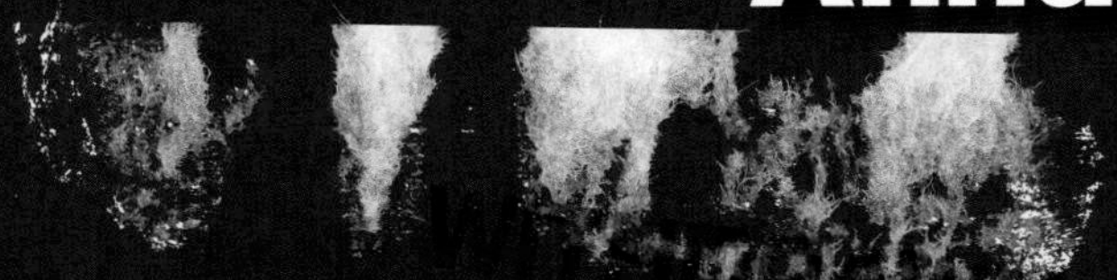

Written by David Clayton

A Grange Publication

ISBN 978-1-908925-45-9

Contents

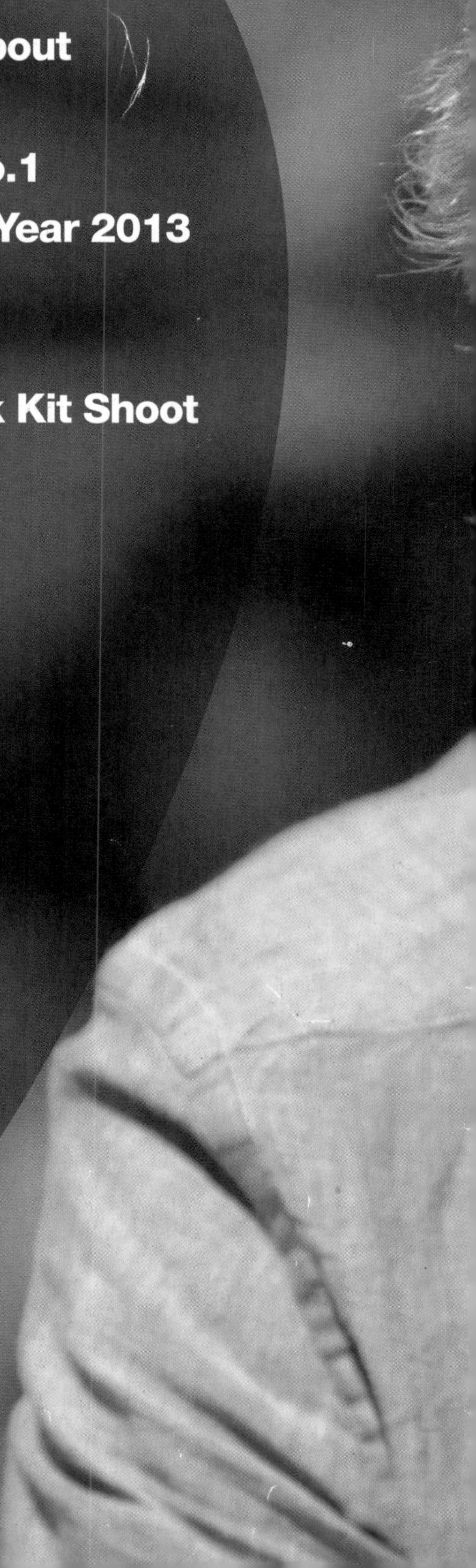

M.C.F.C.
Superbia In Proelio

Season Review in pictures...

We look back at an interesting season for City...

AUGUST:

City began the new campaign with a thrilling 3-2 Community Shield win over Chelsea to add more silverware to the trophy cabinet. Coming from behind to lead 3-1, the Pensioners pulled a late goal back to ensure a nervy end to the Villa Park Clash.

"IT'S ANOTHER TROPHY AND WE PLAYED REALLY WELL. IT'S A GOOD WAY TO START THE SEASON."

PABLO ZABALETA

THE FA COMMUNITY SHIELD
SPONSORED BY McDONALD'S
ETIHAD
AIRWAYS

SEASON REVIEW 2012/13

SEPTEMBER:
New signing Javi Garcia began his City career in perfect style with a towering header in the 1-1 draw at Stoke. The Spaniard almost scored a dramatic late winner, too, during a memorable debut at the Britannia Stadium.

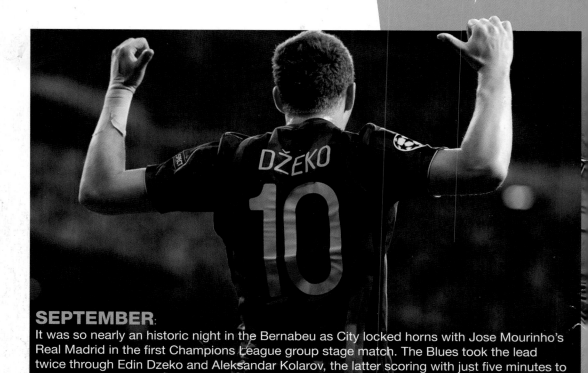

SEPTEMBER:
It was so nearly an historic night in the Bernabeu as City locked horns with Jose Mourinho's Real Madrid in the first Champions League group stage match. The Blues took the lead twice through Edin Dzeko and Aleksandar Kolarov, the latter scoring with just five minutes to go to give City a 2-1 lead. But Karim Benzema and Cristiano Ronaldo dramatically bagged goals in the time that remained to deal City a crushing 3-2 defeat.

OCTOBER

Joe Hart turns in the performance of his life as City cling on against Borussia Dortmund at the Etihad Stadium. The rampant Germans were impossible to contain on the night and Hart made at least four stunning saves before finally being beaten by Marco Reus – and even then he got a hand to the shot! Mario Balotelli rescued a draw in the 90th minute with a penalty but Dortmund proved what a tough group the Blues had found themselves in.

OCTOBER:

Edin Dzeko grabs a dramatic late winner just three minutes from the end of normal time to give City a 2-1 win over Tottenham at the Etihad Stadium. Steven Caulker had headed the visitors ahead on 21 minutes before Sergio Aguero levelled just past the hour – but the Bosnian Diamond had the final word to preserve the Blues' unbeaten Premier League start.

SEASON REVIEW 2012/13

OCTOBER:
Dzeko to the rescue again! With James Milner sent off midway through the first-half and West Brom leading 1-0 with ten minutes remaining, Edin levelled the score within a minute of coming on. He then scored a brilliant winner on 90 minutes to send the travelling fans into a frenzy and secure a 2-1 win over the on-form Baggies.

NOVEMBER:

City secure a 2-0 win over a stubborn Wigan Athletic with a stunning strike from Milner. Balotelli had finally broken the Latics' resolve on 69 minutes and three minutes later Milner struck a howitzer to seal the points at the DW Stadium and keep the Blues in touch with leaders United.

DECEMBER:

With City still reeling from an early Champions League exit and a dramatic last-minute defeat to United in the first derby of the season, December was proving a tough month. Despite an impressive 3-1 win at Newcastle, it seemed more points would be lost in the home game with basement club Reading – until Gareth Barry's injury-time winner saved the Blues' blushes.

JANUARY:

City continued on the road to Wembley with Pablo Zabaleta's 85th-minute winner at Stoke. Having seen off Watford 3-0 in the third round, the Blues enjoyed a terrific start to the New Year and even ended a 38-year jinx at Arsenal with a 2-0 win at the Emirates Stadium. Zaba's goal against the Potters meant the Blues had won six games in a row but there was disappointment to follow…

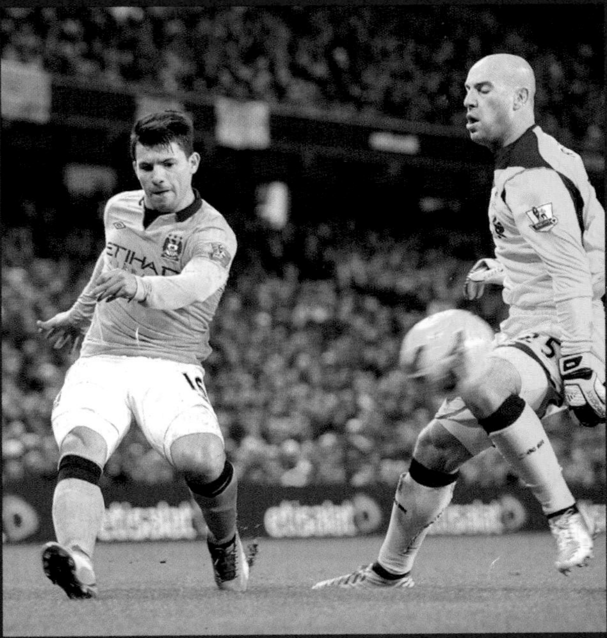

FEBRUARY:

Having failed to see off relegation-threatened QPR at Loftus Road to end the previous month, City then dropped more points in a 2-2 home draw with Liverpool – a game that yielded a contender for Goal of the Season as Aguero somehow equalised from near the corner flag. Then came the season's low point with a demoralising 3-1 defeat to Southampton. Seven points dropped, the Blues' hopes of retaining the title suddenly looked in doubt with United extending their lead at the top to nine points.

SEASON REVIEW 2012/13

MARCH/APRIL:

March had seen City lose further ground in the title race, with Everton perhaps providing the final fatal blow with a 2-0 win at Goodison Park. If the Blues had any lingering hopes of catching the Reds, a win at Old Trafford was a must. If nothing else, City had a point to prove and thanks to goals from Milner and a breath-taking solo effort from Aguero, the Blues triumphed 2-1 to restore local pride and leave the travelling fans wondering about what might have been…

APRIL:

City saw Chelsea off with a 2-1 win at Wembley thanks to goals from Samir Nasri and Aguero to reach a second FA Cup final in three years and pencil in a date with Wigan Athletic. With the Premier League title now gone, the Blues also recorded league wins over Wigan and West Ham at the Etihad but sandwiched in-between was a frustrating 3-1 defeat to Spurs at White Hart Lane.

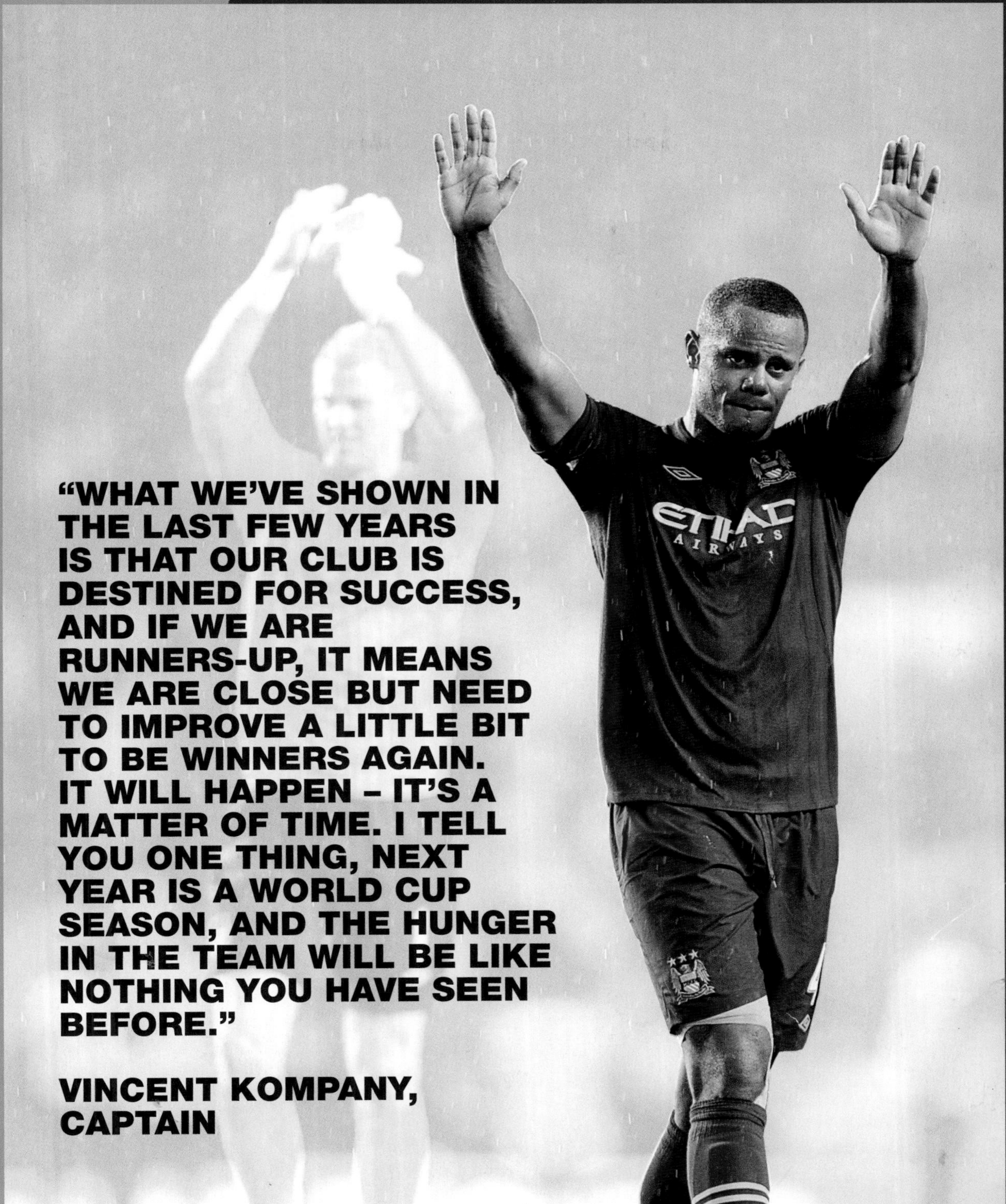

"WHAT WE'VE SHOWN IN THE LAST FEW YEARS IS THAT OUR CLUB IS DESTINED FOR SUCCESS, AND IF WE ARE RUNNERS-UP, IT MEANS WE ARE CLOSE BUT NEED TO IMPROVE A LITTLE BIT TO BE WINNERS AGAIN. IT WILL HAPPEN – IT'S A MATTER OF TIME. I TELL YOU ONE THING, NEXT YEAR IS A WORLD CUP SEASON, AND THE HUNGER IN THE TEAM WILL BE LIKE NOTHING YOU HAVE SEEN BEFORE."

VINCENT KOMPANY, CAPTAIN

MAY:

An off-colour Blues suffer FA Cup Final heartbreak as Ben Watson heads home a 90th-minute winner for Wigan at Wembley. Second position in the Premier League is finally secured a few days later with a 2-0 win at Reading courtesy of goals from Aguero and Dzeko.

Top 10 Goals of the Season

Pick your favourite from these stunning efforts...

01

Sergio Aguero v Liverpool

Aguero never gave up on a long pass towards the corner of the Liverpool box and with Pepe Reina committed to attempting to clear the ball, Aguero coolly knocked it wide of the Spanish keeper before spinning and shooting from a seemingly impossible angle outside of the box to score a truly world class goal.

02

Sergio Aguero v Man United

Another superb individual goal from Aguero and this time, for good measure, it proved to be the winning goal away to Manchester United! Collecting the ball outside the box, Sergio drove forward and past three challenges before powering a rising shot past David De Gea for a goal worthy of winning any match.

03

Carlos Tevez v Wigan

With Wigan stubbornly holding on for a draw – and looking likely to maybe even snatch a shock win – Carlos Tevez popped up with a winning goal with just minutes remaining. Collecting the ball from Aleks Kolarov outside the box, Tevez shielded the ball and then wriggled past two challenges before hitting a shot high into the top corner from 15 yards out.

04

Yaya Toure v Chelsea

One of four Yaya Toure goals in this list, City were desperately looking for a breakthrough against Chelsea and it finally came in the second half. David Silva managed to find Yaya on the edge of the box and he cleverly dropped his shoulder before curling a low shot past Petr Cech who was unsighted by a defender.

05

Yaya Toure v Leeds

A great team goal involving Silva, Tevez and Yaya. Yaya and Silva exchanged passes in midfield before Yaya found Tevez on the edge of the box – Tevez clipped a ball into Yaya's path as he drove into the box and he collected the pass, feigned to shoot before taking the ball round the keeper and slotting it home.

06

Yaya Toure v Ajax

With City on the ropes against the plucky Dutch side, it was Yaya who decided to take the game by the scruff of the neck and lead by example. As a cross came in from the right he controlled the ball at the back post and swivelled all in one movement to bury the ball past the Ajax keeper and bring City back into the game. A classy goal.

07

Aleks Kolarov v Sunderland

A typical Kolarov strike, he curled the ball around with his sweet left foot and into the roof of the net before the Sunderland keeper had even seen it – a spectacular free-kick from the Serbian defender.

08

Yaya Toure v West Ham United

The theory that Yaya only scores spectacular or important goals was underlined by this peach of a shot. The Ivorian picked up the ball on the edge of the box, drifted in a few yards before firing a curling shot into the top left-hand corner that the Hammers keeper had no chance of stopping.

09

Jack Rodwell v Norwich

After a season of frustrating injuries, Rodwell had a fine end to the season. Finally free of the hamstring problems that had blighted his first season at City, Rodwell shone in the last few games and scored twice in the last-day game against Norwich. His first was good but his second was even better, sprinting on to a Yaya Toure pass fully 50 yards before hitting a low shot past the Norwich keeper to make it 2-2.

10

Carlos Tevez v Chelsea

Though Yaya Toure's goal had put City 1-0 up, Chelsea were still well in the game and looking for an equaliser so when sub Tevez picked up a pass from Silva 25 yards out, he took one look up before hitting a cracking shot.

10 things you never knew about... MANUEL PELLEGRINI

01 He was born in Santiago, Chile to Italian parents and his full name is Manuel Luis Pellegrini Ripamonti.

02 His nickname is 'The Engineer' after he picked up a university degree in Civil Engineering at the Pontifical Catholic University in Santiago.

03 Manuel was a one-club player, representing Universidad Chile as a skilful centre-back – he made 451 appearances between 1973 and 1986 for his hometown club.

04 Pellegrini played 28 times for Chile and later became coach of the Chile Under-20 team after retiring as a player.

12

05 He managed 12 clubs before taking over at City and has taken charge of teams in Chile, Ecuador, Argentina and Spain, winning six major titles during his time in South America.

City unveiled new manager Manuel Pellegrini in time for the 2013/14 season – here are some facts about the new Chilean boss...

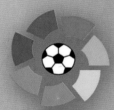

06 He was coach of San Lorenzo when Pablo Zabaleta was still in the youth team at the Argentine club.

07 Pellegrini's longest managerial reign was at Villarreal where he turned an unfashionable small-town club (population 51,000) into Champions League semi-finalists and quarter-finalists during his five years in charge of 'The Yellow Submarine'.

08 Manuel guided Villarreal to finish second in La Liga and, for a time, his team threatened to break the Barcelona/Real Madrid monopoly.

LFP

09 Pellegrini was handed arguably the biggest job in football when he was appointed Real Madrid boss in 2009. Though he lasted only one season in perhaps the most volatile hot-seat in European football, Real accumulated a record number of points – 96 – and only missed out on the La Liga title by three points.

10 Manuel's next club, Malaga, won Champions League qualification in his first season in charge and he came within minutes of taking his team to the semi-finals of the Champions League, conceding two injury time goals to eventual finalists Borussia Dortmund in the second leg of the last quarter final tie.

JOE HART
– City and England No.1!

One of the best keepers in the world, Joe Hart is already one of City's greatest goalkeepers of all time – here are 10 facts you may not have known about Joe...

01 He had won 32 caps for England going into the 2013/14 season and is 98th on the all-time caps list – with plenty of time to catch record holder Peter Shilton who has 125.

02 Joe also won 21 England Under-21 caps.

03 A talented all-rounder, Joe could have had a career in cricket and spent two years in Worcestershire County Cricket Club's youth team.

04 Joe was a substitute for his first club Shrewsbury Town aged just 15! He didn't play and was unused but did eventually make his debut shortly after his 17th birthday.

05 Joe spent time on loan with Birmingham City in 2009/10 – and was voted Blues' Player of the Year.

06 Joe is unique as a top goalkeeper in Europe given he has played in the Conference (non-League), League 2, League 1 and Championship in England – all five top divisions in fact!

07 Joe has kept an incredible 53 Premier League clean sheets over the past three seasons to earn three successive Barclays Golden Glove awards.

08 He has already made 217 starts for City going into the 2013/14 season and is well on his way to breaking many club appearance records given he is still only 26.

09 One of Joe's proudest moments was saving Ronaldinho's penalty against Brazil in February 2013 – England went on to win 2-1.

10 Joe has received plenty of good-natured ribbing for his appearance in a national TV ad campaign for Head and Shoulders, including City fans who ask Joe to 'wash his hair' during quieter periods of home games!

"HE HAS ALREADY MADE 217 STARTS FOR CITY GOING INTO THE 2013/14 SEASON AND IS WELL ON HIS WAY TO BREAKING MANY CLUB APPEARANCE RECORDS GIVEN HE IS STILL ONLY 26"

There was only ever going to be one winner of this award last season...

PABLO ZABALETA was voted 2012/13 Etihad Manchester City FC Player of the Year in association with MCFC Supporters Club (1949) after polling more than two thirds of all the votes registered online.
'Zaba', who joined the Blues from Espanyol in 2008, was the outstanding candidate after a superb season during which he clocked up 42 appearances and scored three goals. He also hit the post three times so was unlucky not to double his tally.
Of course, this only tells half of the story. Never afraid to put his body on the line, Pablo's numerous gashes, bumps and scrapes have endeared him to City fans for whom he has become a cult hero over the past few years.
His never-say-die attitude and the fact he never gives less than his all every time he plays, is dependable, and will always put the team first, are other factors that explain why he has become such an important player for City.
Pablo also wore the captain's armband on numerous occasions in Vincent Kompany's absence and won successive Etihad Player of the Month awards for January and February.
In the ultimate sacrifice for his team, he stopped Wigan's Callum

"I WOULD LIKE TO SAY THANK YOU TO ALL THE CITY FANS WHO VOTED FOR ME. THIS IS A GREAT PERSONAL HONOUR AND SITS ALONGSIDE WINNING THE PREMIER LEAGUE TITLE, CAPTAINING CITY AND PLAYING FOR MY COUNTRY."

McManaman when through on goal – knowing his actions would result in a red card – during the City v Wigan FA Cup Final.
It was typical of the man who has had to battle for his place in the team since arriving five years ago. Interestingly, he was a youth team player when Manuel Pellegrini was manager of his first club San Lorenzo so he will perhaps know the Blues' new manager better than most.
Zaba is also one of the most popular players off the pitch, always having the time to chat with supporters and generally helping anyone he can when asked.
Pablo said: "I would like to say thank you to all the City fans who voted for me. This is a great personal honour and sits alongside winning the Premier League title, captaining City and playing for my country.
"The fans have always been fantastic towards me and shown me a lot of love and respect and I can assure them the feeling is mutual."
He has so far played 193 times for the Blues, scoring seven goals to date, and he represented his country Argentina 30 times by the end of the 2012/13 campaign.
Carlos Tevez made it an Argentine double finishing second with Matija Nastasic finishing third, Edin Dzeko fourth and Sergio Aguero fifth.

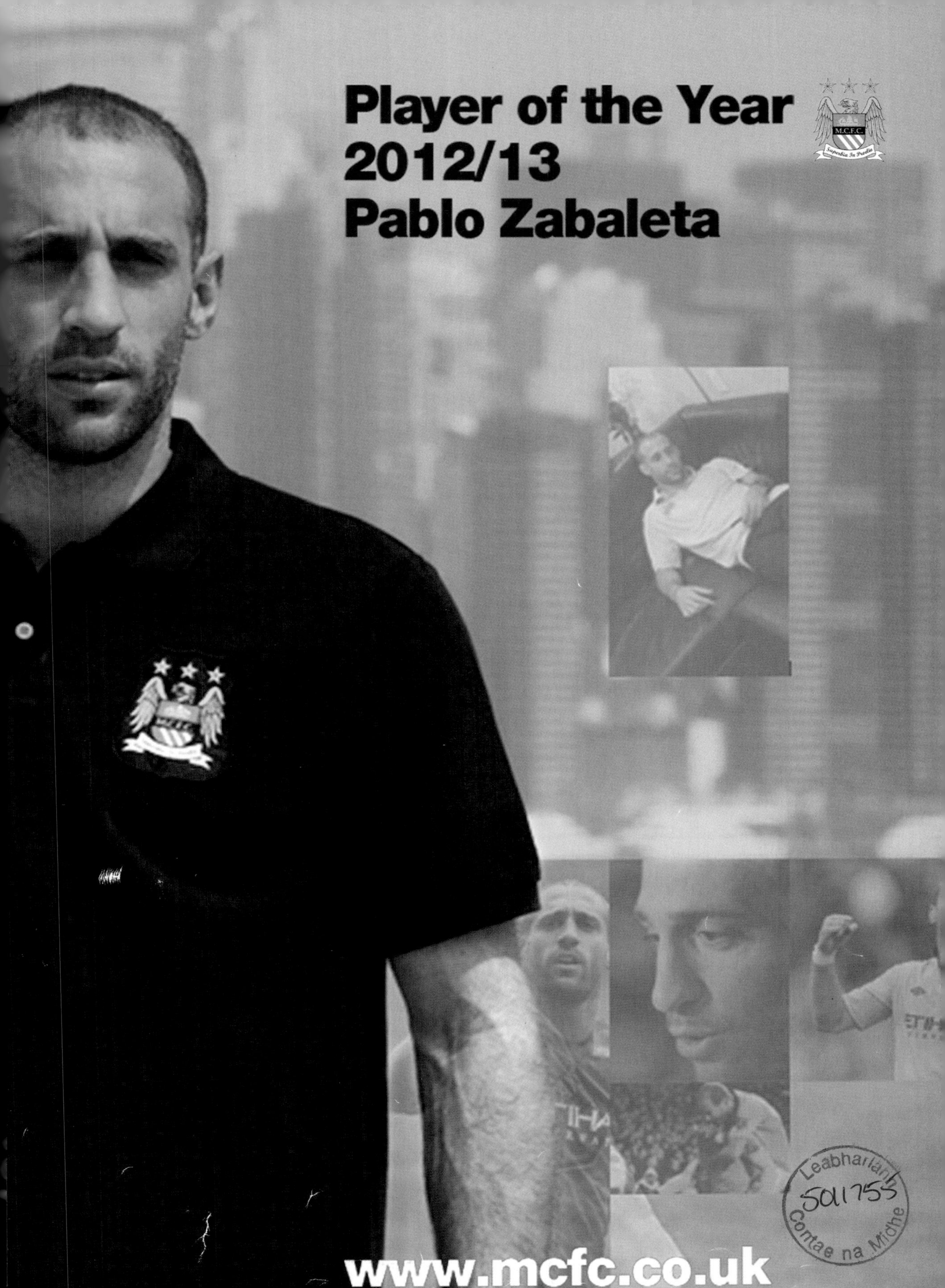
Player of the Year
2012/13
Pablo Zabaleta
www.mcfc.co.uk

David Silva

Wordsearch #1

See how many City-related words you can find in our Wordsearch – remember, the words could be horizontal, vertical or diagonal!

JESUS NAVAS JAMES MILNER ETIHAD STADIUM DAVID SILVA
YAYA TOURE MOONCHESTER SERGIO AGUERO JOE HART
JACK RODWELL GAEL CLICHY

E	T	I	H	A	D	S	T	A	D	I	U	M	B
G	Z	B	R	G	N	K	T	L	J	F	T	R	Y
D	K	C	C	E	Y	T	M	W	Y	W	E	K	A
Z	A	K	Y	K	T	J	K	H	Y	N	K	W	Y
B	H	V	R	M	O	S	C	L	L	S	L	X	A
V	L	K	I	E	Z	I	E	I	C	A	N	D	T
H	G	C	H	D	L	K	M	H	T	V	K	R	O
Z	F	A	G	C	S	S	Z	X	C	A	M	G	U
V	R	G	L	T	E	I	R	C	P	N	Z	C	R
T	F	E	M	M	G	F	L	K	G	S	O	M	E
X	A	M	A	M	D	N	X	V	J	U	W	O	X
G	L	J	N	Z	M	K	L	M	A	S	Y	C	M
T	S	E	R	G	I	O	A	G	U	E	R	O	M
L	L	E	W	D	O	R	K	C	A	J	L	M	P

Answers on page 60/61

GUESS WHO?

Here are six mystery City players – use your powers of observation and detective work to solve their identity....

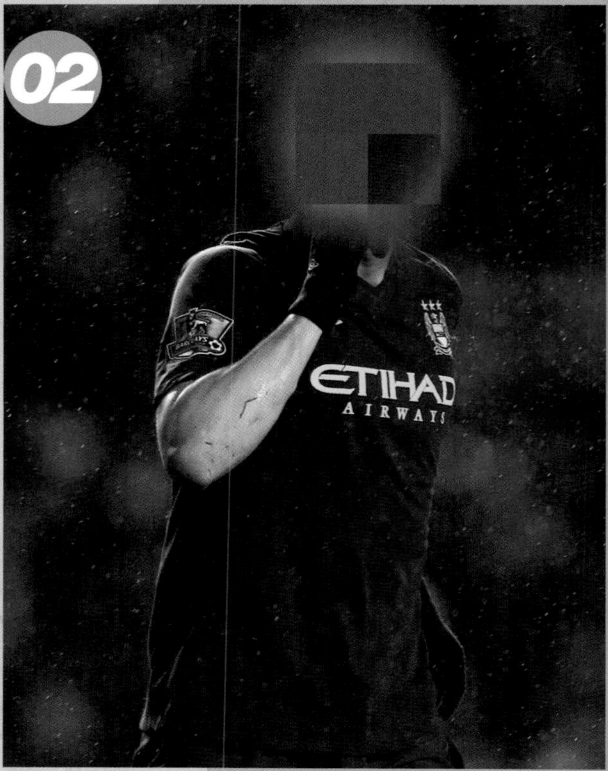

Answers on page 60/61

BEHIND THE SCENES NEW YORK KIT SHOOT

We followed the City players as the new 2013/14 Nike home kit was launched in The Big Apple with our usual access-all-areas photographers...

Matija waiting in the trailer.

Joe puts some tunes on to keep everyone happy.

The guys get their kits on.

Make-up time for Jack.

Waiting for the big shoot.

Vincent leads the guys onto the set.

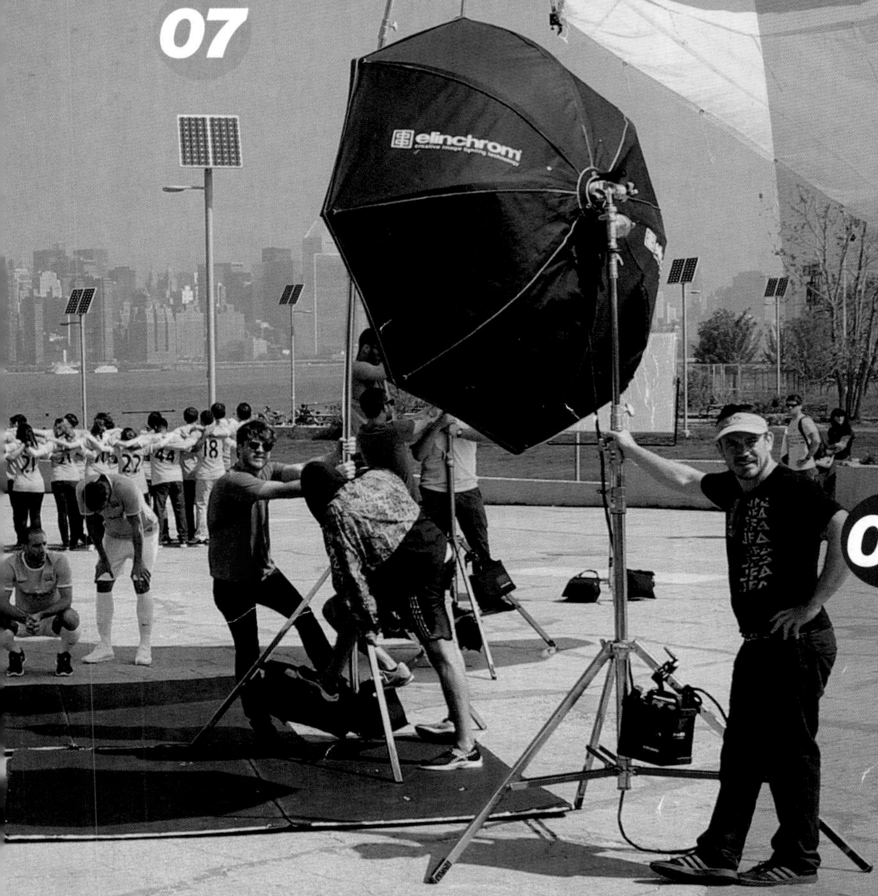

A lot of people for one photograph!

Pablo and Jack pose for the shot.

M.C.F.C.
Superbia In Proelio

JESUS NAVAS

New Player Profile: #1

When Manuel Pellegrini became City's new manager, the first thing he wanted to do was bring pace to his forward line. One player instantly came to his mind – Jesus Navas.

NAVAS, a speedy right winger capable of playing on either flank, had spent his entire playing career at Sevilla where he was something of a crowd idol, exciting the fans at the Ramon Sanchez Pizjuan Stadium for more than eight years.

At 27 years old, Jesus felt the time was right to take on another challenge and, free of the anxiety that blighted his younger years and made it hard for him to travel, he accepted the offer of playing in the Premier League.

City fans love wingers and Navas will enthral the Etihad Stadium with his electric pace and ability to create chances for his team-mates – last season he made 76 opportunities for others via his incisive passing and crosses – and he is also capable of scoring spectacular goals, too.

Navas loves to take on defenders and even the quickest full-backs in England will be nervously looking at when they will face City's speedy wide-man during the 2013/14 campaign.

Navas is a winner, too, having so far collected two UEFA Cups, a UEFA Super Cup, two Copa del Rey titles and the Spanish Super Cup during his time at Sevilla – oh, and not forgetting World Cup and European Championship winners' medals with Spain for whom he has so far won 23 caps.

Navas played 393 times for Sevilla, scoring 34 times and creating countless goals. He will also bring Champions League experience to the Etihad Stadium and hopefully link up well with international team-mate David Silva who says Navas' signing is a great move for the Blues.

"I CAN'T WAIT TO PLAY IN THE PREMIER LEAGUE FOR CITY. THIS IS AN EXCITING MOVE FOR ME AND I AM LOOKING FORWARD TO PLAYING AT THE ETIHAD STADIUM".

Navas said: "I can't wait to play in the Premier League for City. This is an exciting move for me and I am looking forward to playing at the Etihad Stadium.

"We have so many great players and I am coming to Manchester to win titles and obviously the Champions League is a dream of mine."

Shaun Wright-Phillips, Adam Johnson, Peter Beagrie, Peter Barnes and Mike Summerbee – great City wingers from the past – can Jesus Navas add his name to this list? Hopefully, yes!

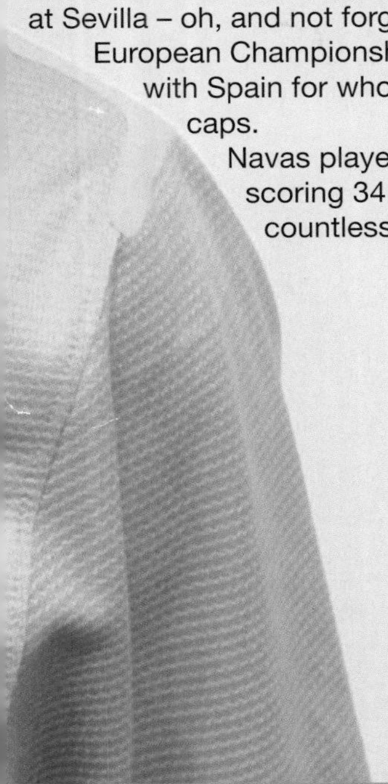

Spot the Difference #1

Can you spot the five differences between picture A and picture B? Circle as many as you can...

Answers on page 60/61

Who is texting?

From the clues contained within the text messages, can you work out who is sending the messages?

AT&T
11:52 PM
100%
"That's three in a row – really happy to collect this award again but couldn't do it without the lads in front of me!"
01

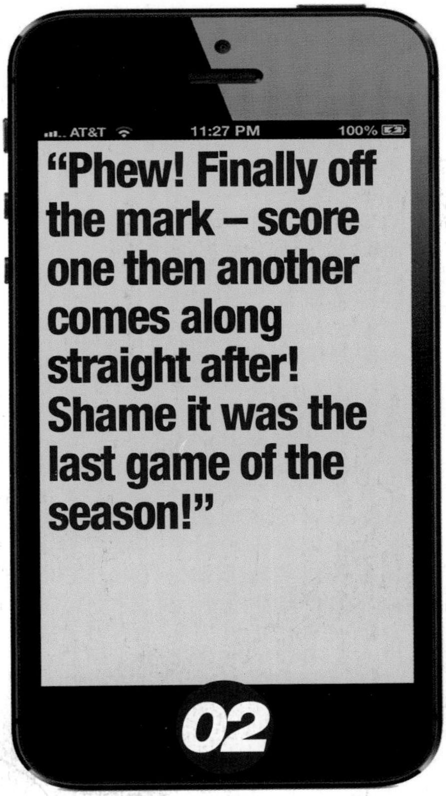
AT&T
11:27 PM
100%
"Phew! Finally off the mark – score one then another comes along straight after! Shame it was the last game of the season!"
02

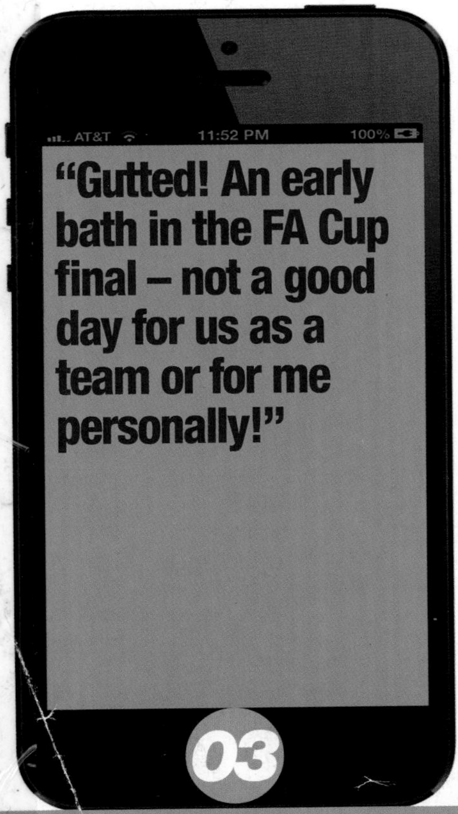
AT&T
11:52 PM
100%
"Gutted! An early bath in the FA Cup final – not a good day for us as a team or for me personally!"
03

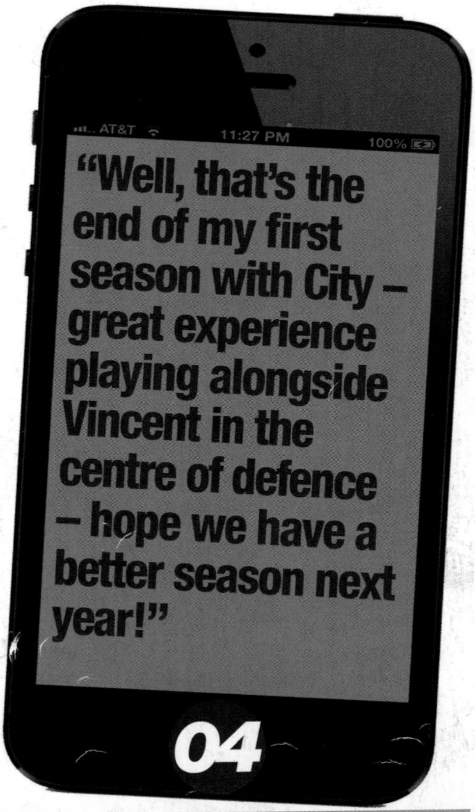
AT&T
11:27 PM
100%
"Well, that's the end of my first season with City – great experience playing alongside Vincent in the centre of defence – hope we have a better season next year!"
04

Answers on page 60/61

Samir Nasri

Crossword

Can you solve the MCFC Annual Crossword 2014? It gets easier the more answers you fill in!

ACROSS

2 What kind of product did Joe Hart promote on TV throughout last season? (7)
4 Which country does Yaya Toure play for? (5,5)
6 Who joined City from Shakhtar Donetsk in summer 2013? (11)
9 Which City player scored two own goals last season? (6,5)
11 From which team did Jesus Navas sign? (7)
14 Who scored the winning goal in the 2-1 win away to Manchester United? (6,6)
15 Which club did Samir Nasri and Gael Clichy join City from? (7)
17 Who drew 2-2 both home and away with City last season? (9)
18 Which country does Matija Nastasic play for? (6)
19 How many Premier League clean sheets did City keep last season? (8)
20 Who did City beat in the FA Cup semi-final in 2013? (7)

DOWN

1 Who was voted the 2013 Player of the Year? (5,8)
3 Who is the new Elite Development Squad Manager? (7,6)
5 Which team from City's Champions League group made it all the way to the Final? (8,8)
7 Which country does Vincent Kompany captain? (7)
8 Which country does Manuel Pellegrini come from? (5)
10 Who scored the most Premier League goals for City last season? (4,5)
12 Joe Hart saved a penalty against which country at Wembley in 2013? (6)
13 Who scored two goals for City on the final day of the 2012/13 season? (4,7)
16 In which city did the Blues launch the new home kit? (3,4)

Answers on page 60/61

THE BIG CITY QUIZ 2014

20 questions to test your City knowledge...

01 WHO SCORED CITY'S LAST GOAL OF THE 2012/13 SEASON?

02 HOW MANY TIMES – INCLUDING CUPS AND FRIENDLIES – DID CITY PLAY CHELSEA DURING THE 2012/13 SEASON?

03 WHICH CITY PLAYER JOINED THE BLUES FROM FIORENTINA IN JULY 2013?

04 WHICH CLUB DID JOE HART JOIN CITY FROM?

05 TRUE OR FALSE? – DAVID SILVA JOINED CITY FROM ATLETICO MADRID…

06 JOE HART WON THE GOLDEN GLOVE AWARD FOR KEEPING THE MOST CLEAN SHEETS IN 2012/13 – HOW MANY OF THESE AWARDS HAS HE NOW WON? 1, 2 OR 3?

07 WHO WERE THE ONLY TWO TEAMS TO WIN AT THE ETIHAD STADIUM IN 2012/13? (1 POINT FOR EACH)

08 WHICH TWO TEAMS FROM
ITY'S CHAMPIONS LEAGUE
ROUP REACHED THE LAST
OUR OF THE COMPETITION?
1 POINT FOR EACH TEAM)

09 HOW MANY TEAMS DID
ITY BEAT HOME AND AWAY
N THE PREMIER LEAGUE
AST SEASON? 6, 7 OR 8?
1 POINT FOR EACH NAMED
EAM)

10 WHICH THREE
HAMPIONSHIP SIDES DID
ITY BEAT ON THE WAY TO
HE 2013 FA CUP FINAL?
1 POINT FOR EACH NAMED
EAM)

11 CITY MASCOT MOONCHESTER HAS A FEMALE COMPANION, CAN YOU NAME HER?

12 WHO ARE THE ONLY TWO SIDES CITY FAILED TO BEAT HOME AND AWAY LAST SEASON AND, FOR A BONUS POINT, WHAT DO BOTH CLUBS HAVE IN COMMON? (1 POINT FOR EACH CORRECT ANSWER)

13 WHICH TEAM DID MATIJA NASTASIC SIGN FROM?

14 WHO ARE CITY'S NEW KIT MANUFACTURERS FOR THE 2013/14 SEASON?

15 WHY DID THE COMMUNITY SHIELD TAKE PLACE AT VILLA PARK LAST SEASON? A) WEMBLEY WAS BEING REPAIRED B) THE OLYMPICS WERE ON C) IT WAS DECIDED IT WAS FAIRER TO BOTH SETS OF FANS

16 HOW MANY TROPHIES DID ROBERTO MANCINI WIN AS CITY MANAGER? (1 POINT FOR EACH TROPHY NAMED)

17 CITY PARTNERED AN AMERICAN BASEBALL TEAM TO FORM NEW YORK CITY FC – WHICH BASEBALL TEAM WAS IT? (2 POINTS)

18 WHO SCORED CITY'S GOALS IN THE 2-1 WIN AWAY TO MANCHESTER UNITED? (1 POINT FOR EACH)

19 WHICH TEAM DID MARIO BALOTELLI JOIN?

20 WHO KNOCKED CITY OUT OF THE 2012/13 CAPITAL ONE CUP?

SCORE CHECKER:

34-28 points – are you after Pellegrini's job? Brilliant!
27-20 points – very good! You know your stuff!
19-10 points – not bad but you could have done better.
09-0 points – stinker! You must improve your knowledge!

Answers on page 60/61

FERNANDINHO...
New Player Profile: #2

City's first signing of the summer was midfielder Fernandinho who signed for the Blues on 6 June 2013.

THE BRAZIL international – full name Fernando Luiz Rosa – joined from Ukrainian side Shakhtar Donetsk, where he'd played for the past eight years and won an impressive 14 winners' medals.
A box-to-box midfielder blessed with an explosive turn of pace, marathon lung power and the ability to break up opposition moves, Fernandinho will provide the energy and verve needed to complement Yaya Toure, James Milner, Javi Garcia and Gareth Barry in the midfield engine room.
Although normally a defensive midfielder, he also possesses a rocket of a shot which has helped him accumulate 68 career goals to date – not bad for someone whose job is to mostly sit in front of the back four!
Fernandinho came up through the youth ranks at Atletico Paranaense in Brazil, making his debut in 2002 as a 17-year old.
In 2003, he went on to feature in Brazil's FIFA World Youth Championship title-winning side in UAE, scoring the winning goal in the final against a Spain side which included future Barcelona legend Andres Iniesta.
Shakhtar took a punt on the 20-year old to join a growing stable of Brazilians at the club, including former City favourite Elano.
It was the 2007/08 campaign when Fernandinho announced himself to the European stage with a series of fine performances in Shakhtar's run to the Ukrainian Cup, scoring 11 goals and winning the Ukrainian league's Golden Football award for best player.
And things got even better for the Londrina-born midfielder in the next campaign when he was an integral member of the team to clinch the UEFA Cup, scoring four goals in nine appearances,

IN 2003, HE WENT ON TO FEATURE IN BRAZIL'S FIFA WOR YOUTH CHAMPIONSHIP TITLE-WINNING SIDE IN UAE, SCORING THE WINNING GOAL IN THE FINA AGAINST A SPAIN SIDE WHICH INCLUDED FUTURE BARCELONA LEGEND ANDRES INIESTA.

including the winner against Spurs in the Round of 16.
He first won international recognition in 2008 when he played in the 3-2 friendly defeat to Germany in Stuttgart, lining up alongside ex-City striker Robinh as well as Neymar and Daniel Alves. Fernandinho – which translated means 'Little Fernando' – played 70 minutes and has since gone on to make another four appearances for Brazil.
His last call-up was in the 2-1 win over Edin Dzeko' Bosnia in February 2012 but he will hope the move to City means he can win a place in the national team in time for the 2014 World Cup in his home country.
One of the highlights of his last season at Shakhtar came on 23 October 2012 when he scored the winner in a 2-1 Champions League group stage wi over Chelsea – one of five goals he netted in his las campaign with the Ukrainians. City will hope he is equally effective in the 2013/14 Champions League campaign.

M.C.F.C.
Superbia In Proelio
ETIHAD

ALVARO NEGREDO
New Player Profile: #3

Alvaro Negredo became Manuel Pellegrini's third signing of the summer when he joined City for an undisclosed fee from Sevilla in July.

THE SPANISH forward represented his country at last summer's Confederations Cup and was believed to have been a target for City since the departure of Carlos Tevez to Serie A Champions Juventus.

Negredo spent four seasons with Sevilla, during which he made 139 appearances and scored 70 goals including an impressive 25 in La Liga last season.

Negredo will form part of an exciting new attack that includes Sergio Aguero and Edin Dzeko. One other player who will be thrilled with Negredo signing with City is Jesus Navas, who played with Negredo at Sevilla and hopefully they will transfer their understanding from La Liga to the Premier League.

Negredo started his career with Rayo Vallecano and made his debut in 2004, where he made 12 appearances scoring once. He only spent one season at the club after moving to the Real Madrid B team before making his senior debut against Atletico Madrid in a friendly. During his time with the Madrid second string, he scored 22 goals in 65 appearances during two seasons with the club before signing a contract with Almeria where he secured regular first team football and scored 32 goals in 73 games.

In 2009 he put pen to paper for a deal with Sevilla, reportedly around £15 million, despite Real Madrid having the option to buy him back in the first two years of his contract. While with Sevilla, he became a firm fan favourite and scored many vital goals for the club. He also made his debut with the Spanish National side shortly after and since his debut for La Roja, he has made 14 caps for his country scoring six goals.

WITH MORE THAN 300 APPEARANCES IN HIS CLUB CAREER, NEGREDO WILL FEEL THAT HE CAN PROVE TO BE A BIG HIT IN THE PREMIER LEAGUE AND HELP SECURE MORE SILVERWARE AT THE ETIHAD.

He also represented Spain at the European Championships in 2012 where he picked up a winners' medal as Spain added another trophy to the World Cup they won two years earlier.

Negredo, 27, will be looking to add to his Copa Del Rey winners' medal in 2010 with more trophies for City. With Spain internationals Navas, Javi Garcia and David Silva already with the Blues, he should find his feet quickly in England.

With more than 300 appearances in his club career, Negredo will feel that he can prove to be a big hit in the Premier League and help secure more silverware at the Etihad.

He will also be hoping that his move to Manchester can help him improve his overall performance and increase the chance for him to represent his country in the World Cup in 2014.

ETIHAD
AIRWAYS
9

Spot the Difference #2

Can you spot the five differences between picture A and picture B? Circle as many as you can...

Answers on page 60/61

Where's Vincent?

We've hidden Vincent amongst the crowd, can you find him?

Joe Hart

Wordsearch #2

Here's another Wordsearch to solve – this time it's about a match day. There are 10 words to find. Remember, the words could be horizontal, vertical or diagonal...

REFEREE CORNER FLAG PROGRAMME HALF TIME CROWD
PITCH PLAYERS DUG OUT MANAGERS SUPPORTERS

E	M	M	A	R	G	O	R	P	E
P	C	R	O	W	D	B	N	M	M
L	E	P	N	K	L	R	I	G	A
A	E	Q	I	Z	L	T	K	D	N
Y	R	R	R	T	F	J	U	W	A
E	E	Y	M	L	C	G	F	M	G
R	F	V	A	C	O	H	T	R	E
S	E	H	Y	U	W	L	C	D	R
S	R	E	T	R	O	P	P	U	S
G	A	L	F	R	E	N	R	O	C

Answers on page 60/61

STEVAN JOVETIC
New Player Profile: #4

Stevan Jovetic joined City from Fiorentina in July 2013. The 23-year-old Montenegro international signed for the Blues after attracting the interest of many of Europe's top clubs.

SOMETHING of a teenage sensation when he first broke into senior football with Partizan Belgrade, he made club history by captaining the team aged only 17.

Jovetic scored 23 goals in 61 games for the Serbian giants before moving to Italy in 2008 for a fee in the region of £8m. He spent three seasons in Serie A with the club nicknamed 'La Viola' (because of their violet-coloured shirts) and became a firm favourite with the Fiorentina supporters.

His five seasons in Florence yielded 40 goals from 134 appearances and he helped his new employers to Champions League qualification for the first time in a decade, though a cruciate ligament injury meant

STEVAN BECAME MANUEL PELLEGRINI'S FOURTH SIGNING OF THE SUMMER AFTER COMPLETING HIS MOVE FROM FIORENTINA IN JULY WHERE HE HAD BECOME ONE OF EUROPE'S MOST COVETED STRIKERS, IMPRESSING FOR CLUB AND COUNTRY.

he missed the entire 2010/11 campaign.

In Europe he has scored two goals each against Liverpool and Bayern Munich during Champions League matches and at international level he captained his country aged 17 at Under-21 level after taking the armband of his idol Marko Vucinic.

He has since represented the senior Montenegro side on 27 occasions, making his debut against Hungary in 2007, and has scored 10 goals to date. He has also played against England in the World Cup qualifiers and is a close friend of former Fiorentina defender Matija Nastasic.

Jovetic wore the No.8 shirt for Fiorentina but with that squad number taken, he has opted for the No.35 shirt at City. Fiorentina supporters gave him the nickname 'Jo-Jo.' His boyhood hero is Ukraine legend and former AC Milan and Chelsea striker Andriy Shevchenko, who Stevan pretended to be during school matches and kick-abouts in the park.

Former Montenegro boss Dejan Savicevic once commented: "He is utterly fearless and I don't see a limit to his potential. Is he the new Savicevic? No, he can be even better. He reminds me of Johan Cruyff."

Stevan became Manuel Pellegrini's fourth signing of the summer after completing his move from Fiorentina in July where he had become one of Europe's most coveted strikers, impressing for club and country.

City had been linked with him for a couple of years and he revealed he joined the Blues because they had shown the most interest in signing him.

Jovetic appeared for Fiorentina 116 times, scoring 35 goals, and will form a new-look City attack that will also feature Sergio Aguero, Alvaro Negredo and Edin Dzeko.

Pablo Zabaleta

Design your own boots!

We've provided the boot, you provide the design! How would you make your boots look if you had the chance...?

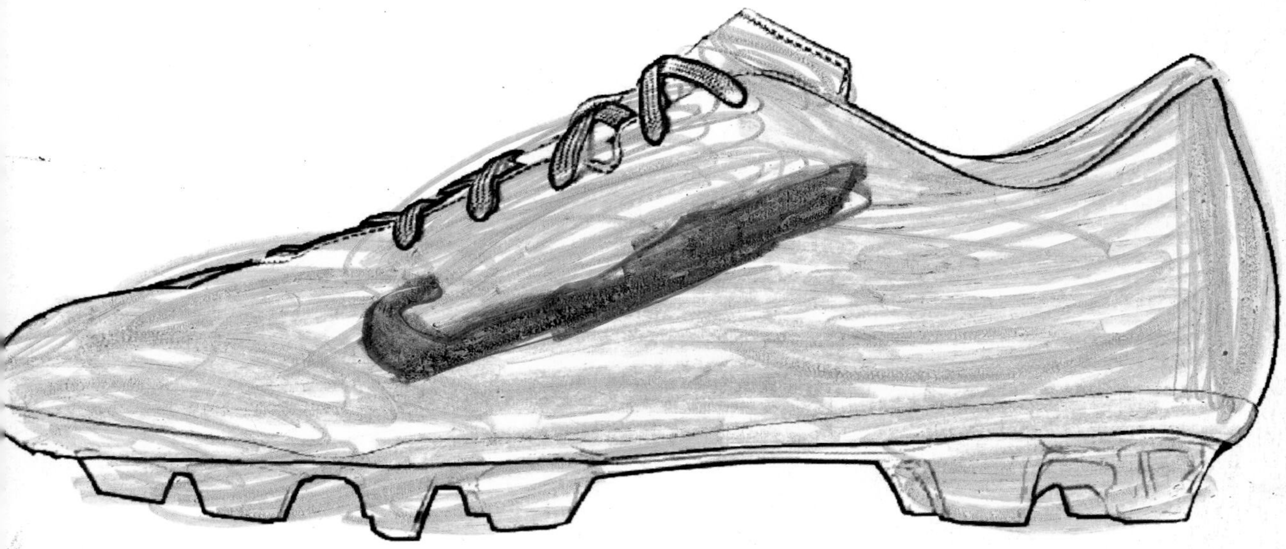

MANCHESTER CITY FC
Squad Profiles 2013/14

NAME: **JOE HART**
POSITION: **GOALKEEPER**
SQUAD NUMBER: **1**

Date of Birth:
19/04/1987

Previous Clubs:
Shrewsbury Town, Tranmere Rovers (loan), Blackpool (loan), Birmingham City (loan)

2012/13 Apps (All Comps):
45 starts

2012/13 Goals (All Comps):
0

NAME: **GAEL CLICHY**
POSITION: **LEFT-BACK**
SQUAD NUMBER: **22**

Date of Birth:
26/07/1985

Previous Clubs:
Cannes, Arsenal

2012/13 Apps (All Comps):
33 starts, 4 sub

2012/13 Goals (All Comps):
0

GOALKEEPER & DEFENCE

NAME: **ALEKSANDAR KOLAROV**
POSITION: **LEFT-BACK**
SQUAD NUMBER: **13**

Date of Birth:
10/11/1985

Previous Clubs: FK Cukaricki Stankom, OFK Beograd, Lazio

2012/13 Apps (All Comps):
17 starts, 13 sub

2012/13 Goals (All Comps):
4

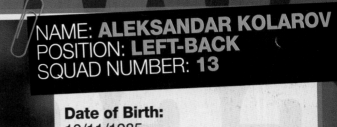

NAME: **PABLO ZABALETA**
POSITION: **RIGHT-BACK**
SQUAD NUMBER: **5**

Date of Birth:
16/01/1985

Previous Clubs:
San Lorenzo, Espanyol

2012/13 Apps (All Comps):
39 starts, 3 sub

2012/13 Goals (All Comps):
3

MANCHESTER CITY FC
Squad Profiles 2013/14

NAME: **MICAH RICHARDS**
POSITION: **RIGHT-BACK**
SQUAD NUMBER: **2**

Date of Birth:
24/06/1988

Previous Clubs:
None

2012/13 Apps (All Comps):
8 starts

2012/13 Goals (All Comps):
0

NAME: **MATIJA NASTASIC**
POSITION: **CENTRE-BACK**
SQUAD NUMBER: **33**

Date of Birth:
28/03/1993

Previous Clubs:
Partizan Belgrade, Fiorentina

2012/13 Apps (All Comps):
30 starts

2012/13 Goals (All Comps):
0

NAME: **VINCENT KOMPANY**
POSITION: **CENTRE-BACK**
SQUAD NUMBER: **4**

Date of Birth:
10/04/1986

Previous Clubs:
Anderlecht, SV Hamburg

2012/13 Apps (All Comps):
37 starts

2012/13 Goals (All Comps):
1

NAME: **JOLEON LESCOTT**
POSITION: **CENTRE-BACK**
SQUAD NUMBER: **6**

Date of Birth:
16/08/1982

Previous Clubs:
Wolverhampton Wanderers, Everton

2012/13 Apps (All Comps):
23 starts, 10 sub

2012/13 Goals (All Comps):
1

MANCHESTER CITY FC
Squad Profiles 2013/14

NAME: **JAMES MILNER**
POSITION: **MIDFIELD**
SQUAD NUMBER: **7**

Date of Birth:
04/01/1986

Previous Clubs:
Leeds United, Swindon Town (loan), Newcastle United, Aston Villa

2012/13 Apps (All Comps):
26 starts, 10 sub

2012/13 Goals (All Comps):
4

NAME: **JACK RODWELL**
POSITION: **MIDFIELD**
SQUAD NUMBER: **17**

Date of Birth:
11/03/1991

Previous Clubs:
Everton

2011/12 Apps (All Comps):
N/A

2011/12 Goals (All Comps):
N/A

MIDFIELD

NAME: GARETH BARRY
POSITION: MIDFIELD
SQUAD NUMBER: 18

Date of Birth:
23/02/1981

Previous Clubs:
Aston Villa

2012/13 Apps (All Comps):
37 starts, 4 sub

2012/13 Goals (All Comps):
2

NAME: YAYA TOURE
POSITION: MIDFIELD
SQUAD NUMBER: 42

Date of Birth:
13/05/1983

Previous Clubs:
SK Beveren, Metalurg Donetsk, Olympiackos, Monaco, Barcelona

2012/13 Apps (All Comps):
42 starts

2012/13 Goals (All Comps):
10

MANCHESTER CITY FC
Squad Profiles 2013/14

NAME: **JESUS NAVAS**
POSITION: **MIDFIELD**
SQUAD NUMBER: **15**

Date of Birth:
21/11/1985

Previous Clubs:
Sevilla

2012/13 Apps (All Comps):
N/A

2012/13 Goals (All Comps):
N/A

NAME: **FERNANDINHO**
POSITION: **MIDFIELD**
SQUAD NUMBER: **25**

Date of Birth:
04/05/1985

Previous Clubs:
Atletico Paranaense, Shakhtar Donetsk

2012/13 Apps (All Comps):
198

2012/13 Goals (All Comps):
36

MIDFIELD

NAME: **SAMIR NASRI**
POSITION: **MIDFIELD**
SQUAD NUMBER: **8**

Date of Birth:
26/06/1987

Previous Clubs:
Marseille, Arsenal

2012/13 Apps (All Comps):
32 starts, 6 sub

2012/13 Goals (All Comps):
5

NAME: **DAVID SILVA**
POSITION: **MIDFIELD**
SQUAD NUMBER: **21**

Date of Birth:
08/01/1986

Previous Clubs:
Valencia, Eibar (loan), Celta Vigo (loan)

2012/13 Apps (All Comps):
38 starts, 3 sub

2012/13 Goals (All Comps):
5

MANCHESTER CITY FC
Squad Profiles 2013/14

NAME: **SERGIO AGUERO**
POSITION: **STRIKER**
SQUAD NUMBER: **16**

Date of Birth:
02/06/1988

Previous Clubs:
Independiente, Atletico Madrid

2012/13 Apps (All Comps):
30 starts, 10 sub

2012/13 Goals (All Comps):
17

NAME: **STEVAN JOVETIC**
POSITION: **STRIKER**
SQUAD NUMBER: **35**

Date of Birth:
02/11/1989

Previous Clubs:
Partizan, Fiorentina

2012/13 Apps (All Comps):
N/A

2012/13 Goals (All Comps):
N/A

NAME: **ALVARO NEGREDO**
POSITION: **STRIKER**
SQUAD NUMBER: **09**

Date of Birth:
20/08/1985

Previous Clubs:
Rayo Vallecano, Real Madrid B, Almeria, Sevilla

2012/13 Apps (All Comps):
N/A

2012/13 Goals (All Comps):
N/A

NAME: **EDIN DZEKO**
POSITION: **STRIKER**
SQUAD NUMBER: **10**

Date of Birth:
17/03/1986

Previous Clubs: Zeljeznicar, Teplice, Usti nad Labem (loan), VfL Wolfsburg

2012/13 Apps (All Comps):
23 starts, 22 sub

2012/13 Goals (All Comps):
15

Us v them

How did our boys do against the rest of the Premier League in the final stats list? Did any of our players top the various lists of 'mosts'...?

ASSISTS:

Top:
Juan Mata 12

City:
David Silva/
Carlos Tevez 8

SHOTS:

Top:
Luis Suarez 143

City:
Edin Dzeko 76

BOOKINGS:

Top:
Luis Suarez
Bradley Johnson
Matthew Lowton
Craig Gardner
Ramires
(10 each)

City:
Pablo Zabaleta 7

INTERCEPTIONS:

Top:
Morgan Schneiderlin 139

City:
Gael Clichy 68

PASSES COMPLETED:

Top:
Mikel Arteta 2517

City:
Yaya Toure 2245

GAMES PLAYED:

Top:
Simon Mignolet
Robin Van Persie
Jussi Jaaskelainen
Seb Larsson
Santi Cazorla
James McCarthy
Jobi McAnuff
Asmir Begovic
Rickie Lambert
Leighton Baines
Jon Walters (38 each)

City:
Joe Hart 38

GOALS FROM OUTSIDE THE PENALTY AREA:

Top:
Gareth Bale 9

City:
James Milner 3

TACKLES:

Top:
Morgan Schneiderlin 146

City:
Pablo Zabaleta 113

WOODWORK STRIKES:

Top:
Robin Van Persie 7

City:
David Silva/
Pablo Zabaleta 3

GOALS:

Top:
Robin Van Persie 26

City:
Edin Dzeko 14

Quiz Answers

SPOT THE DIFFERENCE
(From page 30)

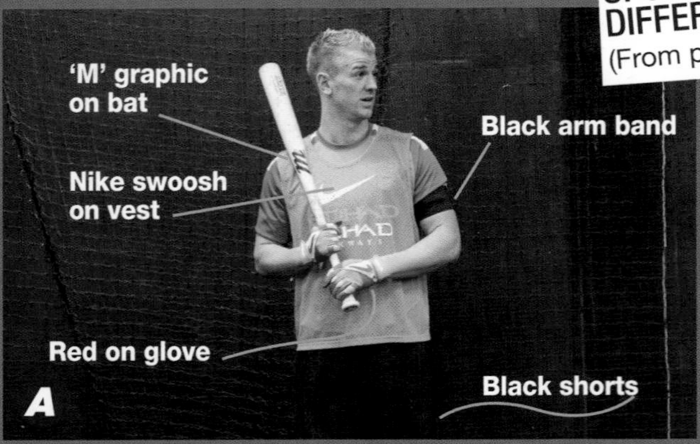

Guess Who?
(From page 24/25)

1 FERNANDINHO

2 EDIN DZEKO

3 DAVID SILVA

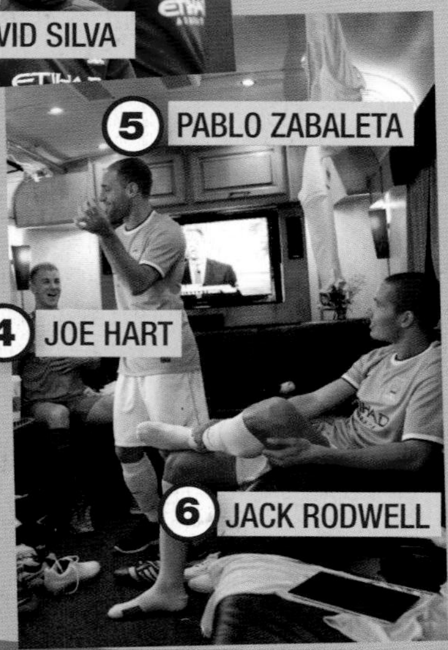
5 PABLO ZABALETA
4 JOE HART
6 JACK RODWELL

WORDSEARCH (From page 23)

E	T	I	H	A	D	S	T	A	D	I	U	M	B
G	Z	B	R	G	N	K	T	L	J	F	T	R	Y
D	K	C	C	E	Y	T	M	W	Y	W	E	K	A
Z	A	K	Y	K	T	J	K	H	Y	N	K	W	Y
B	H	V	R	M	O	S	C	L	L	S	L	X	A
V	L	K	I	E	Z	I	E	I	C	A	N	D	T
H	G	C	H	D	L	K	M	H	T	V	K	R	O
Z	F	A	G	C	S	S	Z	X	C	A	M	G	U
V	R	G	L	T	E	I	R	C	P	N	Z	C	R
T	F	E	M	M	G	F	L	K	G	S	O	M	E
X	A	M	A	M	D	N	X	V	J	U	W	O	X
G	L	J	N	Z	M	K	L	M	A	S	Y	C	M
T	S	E	R	G	I	O	A	G	U	E	R	O	M
L	L	E	W	D	O	R	K	C	A	J	L	M	P

WORDSEARCH (From page 43)

E	M	M	A	R	G	O	R	P	E
P	C	R	O	W	D	B	N	M	M
L	E	P	N	K	L	R	I	G	A
A	E	Q	I	Z	L	T	K	D	N
Y	R	R	R	T	F	J	U	W	A
E	E	Y	M	L	C	G	F	M	G
R	F	V	A	C	O	H	T	R	E
S	E	H	Y	U	W	L	C	D	R
S	R	E	T	R	O	P	P	U	S
G	A	L	F	R	E	N	R	O	C

SPOT THE DIFFERENCE
(From page 40)

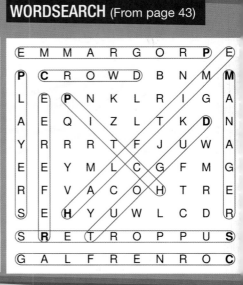

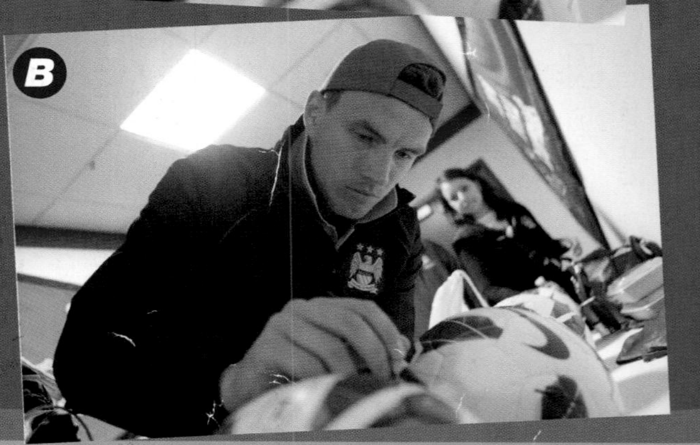

THE BIG CITY QUIZ - ANSWERS

(From page 34/35)

01 JACK RODWELL
02 SIX
03 STEVAN JOVETIC
04 SHREWSBURY TOWN
05 FALSE – IT WAS VALENCIA
06 JOE HAS WON THREE 2011, 2012 & 2013
07 MANCHESTER UNITED AND NORWICH CITY (2 POINTS)
08 BORUSSIA DORTMUND AND REAL MADRID (2 POINTS)
09 SIX – FULHAM, WEST BROM, ARSENAL, READING, ASTON VILLA AND NEWCASTLE (1 POINT FOR EACH CORRECT ANSWER)
10 WATFORD, LEEDS AND BARNSLEY (1 POINT FOR EACH CORRECT ANSWER)
11 MOONBEAM
12 LIVERPOOL AND EVERTON – BOTH FROM MERSEYSIDE (2 POINTS)
13 FIORENTINA
14 NIKE
15 B) THE OLYMPICS
16 MANCINI WON 1 PREMIER LEAGUE TITLE, 1 FA CUP, 1 CHARITY SHIELD – THREE IN ALL (1 POINT FOR EACH CORRECT TROPHY)
17 NEW YORK YANKEES (2 POINTS)
18 JAMES MILNER AND SERGIO AGUERO (1 POINT EACH)
19 AC MILAN
20 ASTON VILLA

Crossword (From page 33)

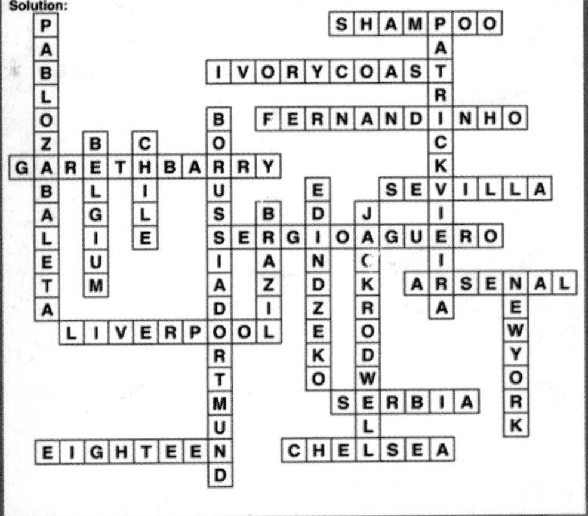
Solution:
PABLOZABALETA
SHAMPOO
PATRICKVIEIRA
IVORYCOAST
FERNANDINHO
BELGIUM
CHILE
GARETHBARRY
BORUSSIADORTMUND
EDINDZEKO
SEVILLA
BRAZIL
JACKRODWELL
SERGIOAGUERO
ARSENAL
NEWYORK
LIVERPOOL
SERBIA
EIGHTEEN
CHELSEA

WHERE'S VINCENT? (From page 41)

WHO IS TEXTING (From page 31)

"That's three in
a row – really
happy to collect
JOE HART
without the lads in
front of me!"
01

"Phew! Finally off
the mark – score
one then an-
JACK RODWELL
last game of the
season!"
02

"Gutted! An early
bath in the FA Cup
final – not a good
PABLO ZABALETA
personally!"
03

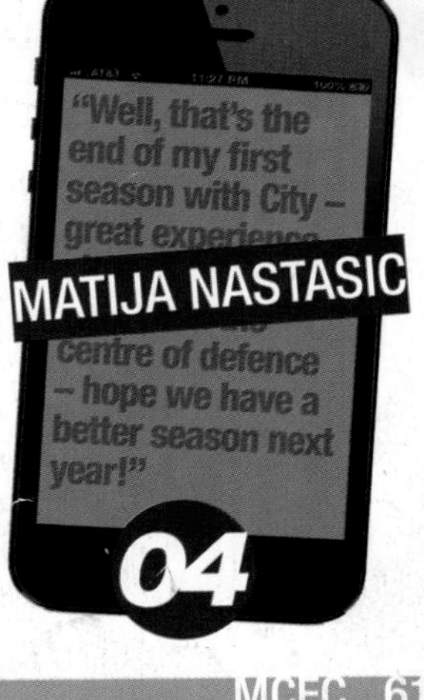
"Well, that's the
end of my first
season with City –
MATIJA NASTASIC
centre of defence
– hope we have a
better season next
year!"
04

ETIHA
AIRWAYS
MADIBA